The Underground Railroad and the Civil War

Untold History of the Civil War

CHELSEA HOUSE PUBLISHERS

Untold History of the Civil War

The Underground Railroad and the Civil War

Albert A. Nofi

CHELSEA HOUSE PUBLISHERS
Philadelphia

The author wishes to thank Gary Collison, author of *Shadrach Minkins: From Fugitive Slave to Citizen* and Derek Schiaronne for their kind advice and assistance. And also Mary S. Nofi for putting up with yet another project.

Produced by Combined Publishing
P.O. Box 307, Conshohocken, Pennsylvania 19428
1-800-418-6065
E-mail:combined@combinedpublishing.com
web:www.combinedpublishing.com

CHELSEA HOUSE PUBLISHERS

Editor in Chief: Stephen Reginald
Managing Editor: James D. Gallagher
Production Manager: Pamela Loos
Art Director: Sara Davis
Director of Photography: Judy L. Hasday
Senior Production Editor: LeeAnne Gelletly
Assistant Editor: Anne Hill

Front Cover Illustration: "Underground Railroad" by Keith Rocco.
Courtesy of Tradition Studios © Keith Rocco

The Chelsea House World Wide Web site address is
http://www.chelseahouse.com

First Printing

135798642

Library of Congress Cataloging-in-Publication Data applied for:
ISBN 0-7910-5434-9

Contents

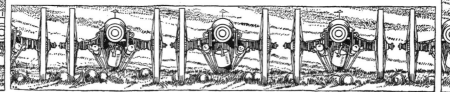

CIVIL WAR
Strategic Theater
1863

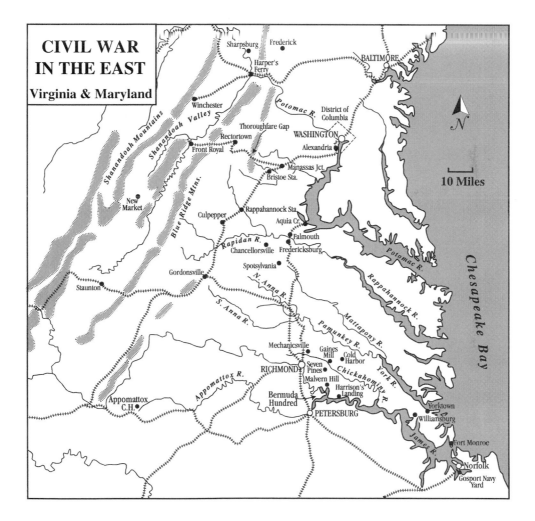

CIVIL WAR IN THE EAST
Virginia & Maryland

Sharpsburg
Frederick
Harper's Ferry
BALTIMORE
Potomac R.
Winchester
District of Columbia
Shanandoah Mountains
Shanandoah Valley
Thoroughfare Gap
WASHINGTON
Rectortown
Front Royal
Alexandria
Manassas Jct.
Bristoe Sta.
Blue Ridge Mtns.
New Market
Culpepper
Rappahannock Sta.
Aquia Cr.
Rapidan R.
Falmouth
Chancellorsville
Fredericksburg
Spotsylvania
Gordonsville
Potomac R.
Staunton
N. Anna R.
Rappahannock R.
S. Anna R.
Mattapony R.
Pamunkey R.
Mechanicsville
Gaines Mill
Cold Harbor
Seven Pines
RICHMOND
Chickahominy R.
York R.
Malvern Hill
Appomattox R.
Harrison's Landing
Appomattox C.H.
Bermuda Hundred
Yorktown
PETERSBURG
Williamsburg
James R.
Chesapeake Bay
Fort Monroe
Norfolk
Gosport Navy Yard

N

10 Miles

Civil War Chronology

1860

November 6   Abraham Lincoln is elected president of the United States.

December 20   South Carolina becomes the first state to secede from the Union.

1861

January-April   Mississippi, Florida, Alabama, Georgia, Louisiana, and Texas also secede from the Union.

April 1   Bombardment of Fort Sumter begins the Civil War.

April-May   Lincoln calls for volunteers to fight the Southern rebellion, causing a second wave of secession with Virginia, Arkansas, Tennessee, and North Carolina all leaving the Union.

May   Union naval forces begin blockading the Confederate coast and reoccupying some Southern ports and offshore islands.

July 21   Union forces are defeated at the battle of First Bull Run and withdraw to Washington.

1862

February   Previously unknown Union general Ulysses S. Grant captures Confederate garrisons in Tennessee at Fort Henry (February 6) and Fort Donelson (February 16).

March 7-8   Confederates and their Cherokee allies are defeated at Pea Ridge, Arkansas.

March 8-9   Naval battle at Hampton Roads, Virginia, involving the USS *Monitor* and the CSS *Virginia* (formerly the USS *Merrimac*) begins the era of the armored fighting ship.

April-July   The Union army marches on Richmond after an amphibious landing. Confederate forces block Northern advance in a series of battles. Robert E. Lee is placed in command of the main Confederate army in Virginia.

April 6-7   Grant defeats the Southern army at Shiloh Church, Tennessee, after a costly two-day battle.

April 27   New Orleans is captured by Union naval forces under Admiral David Farragut.

May 31   The battle of Seven Pines (also called Fair Oaks) is fought and the Union lines are held.

August 29-30   Lee wins substantial victory over the Army of the Potomac at the battle of Second Bull Run near Manassas, Virginia.

September 17   Union General George B. McClellan repulses Lee's first invasion of the North at Antietam Creek near Sharpsburg, Maryland, in the bloodiest single day of the war.

November 13   Grant begins operations against the key Confederate fortress at Vicksburg, Mississippi.

December 13   Union forces suffer heavy losses storming Confederate positions at Fredericksburg, Virginia.

1863

January 1   President Lincoln issues the Emancipation Proclamation, freeing the slaves in the Southern states.

May 1-6	Lee wins an impressive victory at Chancellorsville, but key Southern commander Thomas J. "Stonewall" Jackson dies of wounds, an irreplaceable loss for the Army of Northern Virginia.
June	The city of Vicksburg and the town of Port Hudson are held under siege by the Union army. They surrender on July 4.
July 1-3	Lee's second invasion of the North is decisively defeated at Gettysburg, Pennsylvania.
July 16	Union forces led by the black 54th Massachusetts Infantry attempt to regain control of Fort Sumter by attacking the Fort Wagner outpost.
September 19-20	Confederate victory at Chickamauga, Georgia, gives some hope to the South after disasters at Gettysburg and Vicksburg.

1864

February 17	A new Confederate submarine, the *Hunley,* attacks and sinks the USS *Housatonic* in the waters off Charleston.
March 9	General Grant is made supreme Union commander. He decides to campaign in the East with the Army of the Potomac while General William T. Sherman carries out a destructive march across the South from the Mississippi to the Atlantic coast.
May-June	In a series of costly battles (Wilderness, Spotsylvania, and Cold Harbor), Grant gradually encircles Lee's troops in the town of Petersburg, Richmond's railway link to the rest of the South.
June 19	The siege of Petersburg begins, lasting for nearly a year until the end of the war.
August 27	General Sherman captures Atlanta and begins the "March to the Sea," a campaign of destruction across Georgia and South Carolina.
November 8	Abraham Lincoln wins reelection, ending hope of the South getting a negotiated settlement.
November 30	Confederate forces are defeated at Franklin, Tennessee, losing five generals. Nashville is soon captured (December 15-16).

1865

April 2	Major Petersburg fortifications fall to the Union, making further resistance by Richmond impossible.
April 3-8	Lee withdraws his army from Richmond and attempts to reach Confederate forces still holding out in North Carolina. Union armies under Grant and Sheridan gradually encircle him.
April 9	Lee surrenders to Grant at Appomattox, Virginia, effectively ending the war.
April 14	Abraham Lincoln is assassinated by John Wilkes Booth, a Southern sympathizer.

Union Army
Army of the Potomac
Army of the James
Army of the Cumberland

Confederate Army
Army of Northern Virginia
Army of Tennessee

Henry Brown escaped slavery in a box shipped along the Underground Railroad.

I

Slavery in America

Very early one morning in 1848 a sturdy wooden packing crate arrived at the Pennsylvania Anti-Slavery Society in Philadelphia. It was a large box, three feet long, two feet wide, and two feet eight inches high, and was securely fastened. The box, which came from Richmond, Virginia, was marked "This Side Up With Care."

When the deliverymen had departed one of the officials of the society carefully locked the office door. Then another man knocked on the box, saying "All right?"

From inside the box came the words, "All right, sir."

Within seconds the box was opened. From it emerged Henry Brown, a young fugitive from slavery. As he stepped out of the box, Brown extended his hand and said "How do you do, gentlemen?"

Just 26 hours earlier Henry Brown's friend, Samuel A. Smith, a white shoe dealer in Richmond, had crated him up with a bottle of water and some crackers, and shipped him north by express mail. It had been a difficult journey. The crate first traveled by wagon to a railroad station. It was then loaded on a train which carried it to Washington. In

Washington the crate was shifted to a different train. The second train took it to Baltimore. There it was once again transferred to another train, for the final journey to Philadelphia. It reached Philadelphia at about 2:30 in the morning, and was transferred to a wagon for delivery to the Anti-Slavery Society.

Henry Brown had just taken a ride on the Underground Railroad.

This book is about the most important untold story in American history, the story of the Underground Railroad. The Underground Railroad is about people, mostly quite ordinary people, who at great personal risk worked to right a monstrous wrong—the enslavement of enormous numbers of human beings. These people worked in great secrecy, often in total isolation from one another. They kept few records, and much of what we know about them comes from what is sometimes called "oral tradition," stories passed down from generation to generation. Unfortunately, many of these stories are unreliable. People forgot things or got them mixed up. Sometimes a person just made up or exaggerated a story that soon become part of oral tradition. As historian Larry Gara said in his *The Liberty Line*, "There is probably at least a germ of truth in most of the stories, but unprovable assertions and questionable data" have often made it impossible to separate truth from fiction.

Many of the legends believed and retold about the Underground Railroad are not true. It is not true that quilt patterns were used as "maps" for fugitives on the Underground Railroad; just think of how much time and labor are needed to make a quilt, and how difficult it would be to carry one with you while escaping. Nor was every hidden room in an old building an Underground Railroad hiding place; some

existed to hide smuggled goods or, in colonies where Roman Catholicism was illegal, to hide priests from persecutors. But even without the legends, the real story of the Underground Railroad is certainly an impressive one. Although we will never know the complete history, we do know a lot about it. The bravery, daring, kindness, and sacrifice of many people are not legend but fact. And it is important that what is known be remembered.

The Underground Railroad developed because slavery existed in the United States. By the end of the 15th century there was a small but growing trade in slaves from Africa to the Americas. Over the next 350 years perhaps 15 million Africans were brought to the Western Hemisphere as slaves. Many people died, how many will never be known. Some died in Africa,

Slave auctions like this one were common in the South and spurred the resolve of the abolitionist movement.

13

where some people fought wars to enslave their neighbors. Others died on the "middle passage," the voyage across the Atlantic in crowded, unsanitary vessels. And yet more died in the New World itself, from harsh working conditions, tropical diseases, cruel punishments, or simple despair. The slave trade was not without opposition. The popes, for example, condemned the slave trade on at least five separate occasions. But so great were the profits to be made that most people looked the other way, ignoring moral considerations, religious scruples, or plain decency.

Most of the people brought to the Americas as slaves between the 15th and the 19th centuries went to the West Indies or Brazil. But an estimated 500,000 were brought to what we now know as the United States. The first African slaves to reach what would become the United States arrived with the earliest Spanish explorers, in Puerto Rico, Florida, and the southwest. The first to reach the English colonies along the eastern seaboard were 19 people who landed in Virginia in 1619. The number of African slaves grew slowly at first, but by the time of the American Revolution, 150 years later, about 10 percent of the people in the original 13 colonies were slaves.

Of course the enslaved people tried to resist bondage. They did this in many ways. One was to do as little work as possible, being careful to avoid punishment for laziness. Pretending to be sick was also a useful trick. Sabotage—damaging the master's goods—was another. Some more determined slaves tried to rebel, but slave uprisings always failed. For most, the best way to oppose slavery was to escape. Escape was not easy, but, if successful, the person was free. No one knows who the first slave in the 13 colonies to succeed in escaping was. Whoever it was probably did so by fleeing to the Indians, who lived

just beyond the frontier of settlements in the Appalachian mountains or the swamps of the Carolinas and Florida. Although some Native Americans were themselves slaveholders, others welcomed fugitives. But the frontier kept moving westward, which made safety increasingly difficult to reach.

Fugitive slaves ford a river on their way to freedom.

Escape became easier with the rise of the abolitionist movement shortly before the American Revolution. Abolitionism was aimed at ending—abolishing—slavery. It arose in Europe and America in the mid-1700s. People became abolitionists for many reasons. Religious belief was one, and some religious groups—Quakers, Methodists, and Mennonites, among oth-

Correspondence Along the Underground Railroad

Elijah F. Pennypacker

Letter from E. F. Pennypacker to William Still (one of the conductors at the Philadelphia depot of the Underground Railroad), November 11, 1857.

Wm. Still: Respected Friend,

There are three colored friends at my house now, who will reach the city by the Phil. & Reading train this evening. Please meet them.
We have within the past 2 mos. Passed 43 through our hands, transported most of them to Norristown in our own conveyance.

Thine, etc.
E. F. Pennypacker

★ ★ ★

Letter from Thomas Garrett to William Still, July 19, 1856.

Respected Friend, William Still:

I now have the pleasure of consigning to thy care four able-bodied human beings from North Carolina, and five from Virginia, one of which is a girl twelve or thirteen years of age, the rest all men. After thee has seen and conversed with them, thee can determine what is best to be done with them. I am assured they are such as can take good care of themselves. Elijah Pennypacker, some time since, informed me he could find employment in his neighborhood for two or three good hands. I should think that those from Carolina would be about as safe in that neighborhood as any place this side of Canada. Wishing our friends a safe trip. I remain thy sincere friend,

Thos. Garrett

ers—were soon very important in the movement. Other people became abolitionists because of their belief in the "Rights of Man" or their horror at the inhumanity of slavery. All kinds of people became abolitionists, men and women, black and white, rich and poor, religious and irreligious, famous—such as Benjamin Franklin—and unknown. In addition to working for the abolition of slavery, they began to help people who were trying to flee from bondage. Of course there had always been people willing to help slaves escape, or at least look the other way. But with the rise of the abolitionist movement, escaping from slavery became a little easier.

Many good people in the North and South helped create a network of stations, hiding places, and transportation for the fleeing slaves.

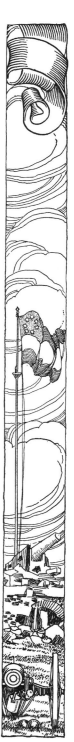

II

The Rise of the Underground Railroad

The Underground Railroad existed long before it received its name. After all, people began escaping from slavery in the United States long before railroads were invented. As early as the 1680s there seem to have been loosely organized networks of people—free and slave—who helped fugitives escape. Although these networks remained very loosely organized, over the next 150 years they grew larger and more skillful. The phrase "Underground Railroad" came into existence in the 1830s, about the time that real railroads began to spread across the country. Tradition has it that the first use of the phrase occurred in 1831. Supposedly, a slave owner was pursuing a fugitive named Tice Davids, who was trying to swim the Ohio River. He saw Davids wade out of the water at the town of Ripley, Ohio—and never saw him again. Although the slave owner searched the town and questioned the townsfolk, he could find not a trace of his slave, and returned in disgust to Kentucky. When

A wagon load of slaves makes its way to freedom.

asked what happened, he is said to have replied, "He must have gone by an underground road."

Whether the tale of Tice Davids is true or not, the phrase "Underground Railroad" was a convenient one, for it described a secret network by which fugitive slaves could travel to freedom in safety. Soon other railroading terms came into use. A guide was called a "conductor," fugitives were called "passengers," and people who donated goods and money to support the system were called "stockholders." Places where fugitives could hide—like "safe houses" in spy stories—were called "stations." However the phrase "Underground Railroad" and the use of other railroading terms is misleading. Although the slave owners thought otherwise, the Underground Railroad was not as organized as its name suggested. It was actually a very loose network of people willing to help others escape from slavery. Sometimes one person "worked" for the Underground Railroad for many years, aiding dozens, hundreds, and in some cases even thousands of people in their escape from slavery. But many people helped just one fugitive escape, and perhaps never realized that by doing so they became part of the history of the Underground Railroad.

There was no typical Underground Railroad worker. In the North most of the workers were members of antislavery societies, of which there were over 2,000 by the 1830s, with over 200,000 members. But many others did not openly advertise their opposition to the institution. In the South, of course, it was unusual for anyone to openly oppose slavery, lest they be beaten or murdered. Many Underground workers were African Americans, some free, some slave, others were white or Native American. An Underground Railroad worker might be a farmer, or a doctor or minister, a sea captain or housewife, a bartender or peddler, a teacher or tradesman. There were cases of slave owners and even slave traders who were secretly conductors on the Underground Railroad.

People supported the Underground Railroad for many reasons. Opposition to slavery was one. But there were others. Many Northerners who were not particularly opposed to slavery decided to support the Underground Railroad because of the Fugitive Slave Law of 1850. The first Fugitive Slave Law had been passed in 1793. It required the officials of any state to assist in the recovery of slaves who had escaped from another state. But it was largely ignored in the North. Southerners who managed to locate their escaped slaves in a Northern state often found that the local people made it difficult for them to claim their "property." Northern sheriffs sometimes arrested slave catchers on technicalities, such as violations of local firearms laws. Northern judges sometimes took so long to examine the slave owner's documents that fugitives had time to flee elsewhere. But the Fugitive Slave Law of 1850 was different. It required officials of the federal government to assist in the recovery of escaped slaves. This offended a lot of people in the North, even those who were not abolitionists. They felt that the new law violated the right of the people of a state to decide whether it should be slave or free. Then, in 1857, there was the Dred Scott Decision. In this decision the Supreme Court basically concluded that no state could bar slavery, if a slave owner chose to move there. This led to still more people who had not sympathized with the antislavery movement beginning to support the Underground Railroad.

Sometimes people supported the Underground Railroad for personal reasons. The children of slave owners often had slave playmates, and in later life there were cases where the master's children helped their former playmates escape. In states that prohibited the freeing of slaves, a master sometimes arranged for some of his slaves to "escape" as a way of granting them their freedom. Even solidly pro-slavery types might sometimes aid an escape as a result of a particular injustice, such as when someone was selling slaves as prostitutes. A few people seem to have worked for the Underground Railroad because it offered them an adventurous life. And there were some who did it for the money that black freemen in the North would pay to get their relatives out of slavery in the South.

But escaping from slavery was hard.

Although there were instances of escapes by whole families, in fact about 80 percent of those who escaped were men aged from about 16 to about 40. They usually fled alone or in small groups. Flight was often undertaken without much planning, particularly if a person discovered that he was about to be sold. Even if they themselves did not want to escape, other slaves often aided those trying to escape. They supplied

A lone slave flees on horseback. Escape from the Deep South was especially difficult because it was a long way to freedom in the North.

food, sometimes hid the person where slave catchers were not likely to go searching, and sometimes even concealed the fact that someone was missing for many days. Slaves who could read and write often helped escapees by forging passes and "freedom papers." Another way that slaves helped their fellow slaves to escape was by supplying information. Through the "slave telegraph," informal contacts with other slaves, people could gather useful information about the surrounding area. So some slaves knew who in their community was likely to help a runaway. And others, often trusted slaves who accompanied the master when he went hunting, usually knew secret paths through nearby forests and swamps. All this information could be conveyed to prospective fugitives.

There were patterns to the ways in which people escaped. The largest proportion of successful escapes were made from Virginia, Kentucky, and especially Maryland (a quarter of all escapes seem to have been from that one state alone). These were the slaves who could follow the Big Dipper to the relative safety of the nearby free states of the North. Slaves who lived near the coasts or along the great rivers—the Mississippi, the Tennessee, and the rest—were sometimes able to escape by water. In Texas, Arkansas, and Missouri slaves occasionally escaped by fleeing to the Indians. Slaves held in the interior areas of the "Deep South" (the Carolinas, Georgia, Florida, Alabama, Mississippi) were the least likely to succeed in escaping, for those areas were far from the free states. But even in these areas, some people managed to escape, sometimes fleeing into swamps such as the Belle Isle Swamp in Georgia, the delta country of Mississippi, or the bayous of Louisiana. Others escaped into the Appalachian Mountains. In these wild areas fugitives often remained free for years, sometimes even forming small communities.

People escaped from slavery in numerous ways. A lone man or a small group fleeing on foot, hiding by day and traveling by night, was probably the most common form of escape. Hiding on a train or in a ship, often with the cooperation of the crew, was another. Some slaves escaped by stealing boats and rowing or sailing their way to freedom. Although Henry "Box" Brown's escape concealed in a wooden crate seems unusual, there were others who found freedom in this fashion. Many others escaped by being hidden in secret compartments built into wagons and carriages. Often people adopted disguises. Fugitives sometimes made themselves look older or younger. Men sometimes dressed like women, or women like men. Some fugitives even escaped disguised as white people. Many slaves used false papers to aid in their escape, including forged passes, letters, and freedom papers. The most famous of all fugitive slaves, Frederick Douglass "stole" himself from his master. He borrowed a sailor's papers, put on seaman's clothing, and boarded a train from Maryland to Philadelphia. Some slaves even escaped from one part of the South to another, using false freedom papers to live openly. And a few even managed to escape "disguised" as slaves, to be led in chains to safety by a "slave trader" who was actually a conductor on the Underground Railroad.

How many people tried to escape and failed will never be known. Sometimes fugitive slaves were killed by their pursuers, or drowned while trying to swim a river, or died from disease while fleeing through swamps or cold weather. Many

This black woman, Maria Weems, escaped dressed in male clothing.

fugitives were quickly recaptured and returned to slavery. Often cruelly punished, they were usually sold far away from their families and friends. Free black people who aided fugitives were often sold as slaves. Whites captured helping fugitives usually received long prison sentences, 10 years for each person whom they had aided being common; Samuel A. Smith, who had crated up Henry Brown and shipped him to freedom, was later caught and spent eight years in prison. At the end of the Civil War scores of people imprisoned for "slave stealing" were released from Southern jails.

Just as we will never know how many people tried but failed to escape from slavery, so we will never know how many succeeded in escaping.

By 1830 the slaveowners were claiming that 30,000 fugitives were living in the North. By 1850 their claims had reached 50,000. In 1850 some slaveowners were estimating the number of fugitives since 1810 at 100,000. Whether the figures were accurate or not, abolitionists circulated these figures, for they proved

Correspondence Along the Underground Railroad

Grace Anne Lewis

Letter to William Still from Grace Anne Lewis, October 28, 1855.

Esteemed Friend,

This evening a company of eleven friends reached here, having left their homes on the night of the 27th, and left there, in the town, their two carriages, drawn by two horses. They went to Thomas Garrett's by open day-light and from thence were sent hastily onward for fear of pursuit. They reached Longwood meeting-house in the evening, at which place a Fair Circle had convened, and stayed a while in the meeting, then, after remaining all night with one of the Kennet Friends, they were brought to Downingtown early in the morning, and from thence, by daylight, to within a short distance of this place.

They come from New Chestertown, within five miles of the place from which the nine lately forwarded came, and left behind them a colored woman who knew of their intended flight and of their intention of passing through Wilmington and leaving their horses and carriages there.

I have been thus particular in my statement, because the case seems to us one of unusual danger. We have separated the company for the present, sending a mother and five children, two of them quite small, in one direction, and a husband and wife and three lads in another, until I could write to you and get advice if you have any to give, as to the best method of forwarding them, and assistance pecuniarily, in getting them to Canada. The mother and children we have sent off of the ususal route, and to a place where I do not think they can remain many days.

We shall await hearing from you. . . .

Very Respectfully,
G. A. Lewis

that the Underground Railroad was a great success. Unfortunately, these numbers cannot be confirmed. For example, it was often said that 40,000 fugitives were living in Canada. But the black population of Canada included many people who had never been slaves. A more reliable estimate was made by William Still. Still, the freeborn son of a fugitive slave, worked for the Pennsylvania Anti-Slavery Society and was one of the most famous managers of the Underground Railroad. After the Civil War, Still wrote what is considered the single most valuable book on the Underground Railroad, even today. In it Still estimated that between 1845 and 1860 about 15,000 people had succeeded in escaping from slavery. So by Still's estimate about 1,000 slaves had successfully escaped each year. Still's estimate is not too different from the average of about 900 escapes a year based on the number of escapees reported to the Census Bureau in 1850 and 1860, the only years in which such information was requested. In 1850, 1,011 fugitive slaves were reported, and 10 years later 803. Allowing for escapes which were never reported, or which the Underground Railroad did not know about, and considering the whole period of slavery in the 13 colonies and the United States, it seems very likely that many more than 100,000 people succeeded in fleeing from slavery by the outbreak of the Civil War.

Frederick Douglass was a prominent leader of the abolitionist movement and the Underground Railroad.

III

The People of the Underground Railroad

*B*ecause of the great secrecy in which they worked, we will never know how many people were involved in the Underground Railroad—thousands certainly, probably tens of thousands. Most were very ordinary, some—Frederick Douglass, John Brown, Lucretia Mott—were famous as authors, lecturers, and leaders of the abolitionist movement. All sorts of people worked for the Underground Railroad, even slave owners who had decided that something had to be done to end the evil institution. Some people did the dangerous work, acting as conductors and stationmasters. But others helped raise money, fought against slavery in the courts, or provided goods. Most of these people worked in secrecy, especially those serving as conductors and stationmasters. Probably a majority of those who worked for the Underground Railroad are unknown. But we do know about a few of them and recount just some of their stories here.

Harriet Tubman (left) poses with a group she led from slavery.

Harriet Tubman was the most famous of all conductors on the Underground Railroad. She was born in 1821, in Maryland to slave parents, who named her Araminta Ross. She grew up working as a field hand on a plantation. In 1843, she married John Tubman, a fellow slave. The marriage was not a happy one.

In 1849, learning that she was about to be sold, Araminta Tubman left her husband and slavery forever, fleeing northward and adopting the name Harriet. She was soon involved with various Quaker antislavery groups and became active in the Underground Railroad. Over the next decade Tubman conducted 19 hazardous missions into the South, mostly to Maryland and Virginia. Some estimates place the number of people she led to freedom at over 300. Among them were several of her brothers and sisters, and both her parents, whose rescue was particularly difficult, for both were in failing health. There were few more effective conductors on the Underground Railroad than Harriet Tubman.

Slaveowners hated Tubman. They posted rewards for her capture. In one case the reward was $12,000, about $300,000 in today's money. But she was a small woman, very plain in appearance, who often wore men's clothes. With her ability to act and speak like a slave, she was so effectively disguised that she was always able to avoid capture. Physically very strong, she was a tough, determined woman, who could be ruthless if necessary. At least once Tubman threatened to shoot an escapee who wanted to turn back, saying "We got to go free, or die." On other occasions, she administered dangerous knock-out drops to young children, lest their crying alert slave catchers to the presence of the fugitives. But she had a gentler side too, and would sometimes use her beautiful singing voice to calm panicky fugitives.

Tubman quickly became a legend among the slaves, who nicknamed her "Moses" because she would lead them out of bondage. Although well-known in the abolitionist community, Tubman never held a formal position with any organization. Between expeditions into the south, she supported herself by working. She gave lectures and "wrote" articles, dictating what she wished to say to a secretary, since she could neither read nor write. Tubman also worked as a cook, often at the summer resort city of Cape May, New Jersey. Perhaps it amused her to do this, for many slave owners spent their summers there, and never knew that the woman for whom they had offered large sums of money was so close at hand.

At the outbreak of the Civil War, Tubman went to the Carolina Sea Islands, where she served the black community by helping to build a school and working as a nurse. She soon began working with the Union army, serving as a spy and scout, and on several occasions guided troops through swamps and forests during military operations. After the war she continued to work for the rights of black Americans and founded a home for poor black freemen. She died in 1913.

Thomas Garrett was a practicing Quaker who spoke using "thee" and "thou" and wore the traditional black clothing of his faith. He was born in Pennsylvania in 1783, the year America won its independence. In 1807 a free black woman who worked for his parents was kidnapped by slave catchers. Garrett went after them and was able to free her before the kidnappers could drag her into the South. That began his ties to the Underground Railroad.

In 1822 Garrett settled in Wilmington, Delaware, a state in which slavery was legal, though there were actually very few slaves. While running a successful iron and steel business, Garrett also began helping runaways, whom he called "God's poor." He soon became one of the most effective stationmasters on the Underground Railroad. He worked closely with William Still, who kept a tally of the people whom Thomas Garrett aided—it came to about 2,700.

Garrett's station operated very much like most other Underground Railroad stations. A conductor would contact him, as "a friend with friends." At times Garrett would shelter the fugitives for just a few hours. Other times he would hide them for several days. He hid fugitives in his house or on other property he owned, or with other sympathetic people. The time a group of passengers remained with Garrett, how he chose to conceal them, and where he hid them depended on several things. Slave catchers might be in the area, making it dangerous for fugitives to move,

or perhaps arrangements for them to pro-
ceed on the next stage of their journey had
been planned in advance. Sometimes he
hired a boat and a boatman to take the
fugitives to safety by water, or got them on
a train, or provided a wagon and driver.
The important thing was that they make
their way safely across the state line into
Pennsylvania. He usually provided the
fugitives with clothing, shoes, food, and
money to help them on their way. This
was costly work, even for a prosperous
businessman like Garrett. But the
Underground Railroad relied on dona-
tions of money and supplies from citizens, churches,
and antislavery organizations, such as the "Women's
Anti-Slavery Sewing Society of Cincinnati," which
made clothing for runaways.

Thomas Garrett was one of the best stationmasters on the Underground Railroad.

Unlike many Underground Railroad workers,
Garrett made no secret of his hostility to slavery. As a
result, supporters of slavery kept their eyes on him.
His activities sometimes got him into trouble. Once a
slave owner threatened to shoot him. But Garrett
responded by saying "Here I am, thee can shoot me if
thee likes." The man backed down.

In 1848 Garrett was convicted of aiding fugitive
slaves. On this occasion he was fined $5,400, about
$150,000 in modern money, and he was forced to sell
much of his property. Despite this he remained an
ardent friend of the fugitive slave, saying " . . . I
haven't a dollar in the world, but if thee knows a fugitive anywhere on the face of the earth who needs a
breakfast, send him to me." With the help of friends in
the antislavery movement, he was soon back on the
job, operating a station on the Underground Railroad.
The last passengers to pass through Garrett's station

Josiah Henson's story inspired Harriet Beecher Stowe (above) to write the famous book Uncle Tom's Cabin.

did so in 1863, shortly after the Emancipation Proclamation. Thereafter, in declining health, Garrett worked for equal rights not only for black Americans but also for women. He died in 1871 and was given a splendid funeral.

Josiah Henson was a fugitive slave who not only returned to the South to rescue others, but provided the inspiration for one of the most important books in American history. He was born into slavery in Maryland in 1789. After passing through a series of owners, he ended up on a plantation near Rockville. As a boy Henson wanted to learn to read. By selling apples he raised 11 cents and bought a copy of *Webster's Speller* and began to teach himself to read. The first words he wrote, tracing them in charcoal, were "Isaac Riley," his master's name. But Riley took a dim view of slaves reading. He beat Henson and put an end to his effort to learn to read. Despite this, over the years "Sie," as young Henson was nicknamed, became a trusted retainer of the Riley family. He was often taken on business trips by his master, and sometimes was even sent alone on long journeys to attend to the master's business. Meanwhile he became a Methodist preacher, and tended to the spiritual needs of the Riley slaves. He was once credited with calming a potentially disastrous outbreak by some 400 slaves. As a trusted slave, Henson was allowed to work in his spare time, and to save money. In 1828 he had enough cash to buy his freedom and that of his wife and child. They settled in Kentucky.

Soon afterward, Riley began to ask for more money. Henson feared that his former master was about to double-cross him. Rather than take the chance that Riley would claim he had never freed the Hensons, in 1830, he fled with his family. It was a difficult journey, but, aided by the Underground Railroad and some friendly Indians, the family made it to Canada.

In Canada Henson prospered and learned to read. He began to help other fugitive slaves, hundreds of whom arrived in Canada each year. Henson helped start a school for the "Coloured [sic] inhabitants of Canada." And he became a conductor on the Underground Railroad. Between 1835 and 1840 Henson made several journeys into the South, and is credited with helping about 200 slaves escape. In 1840 Henson visited England, where he was introduced to Queen Victoria and the archbishop of Canterbury. When the archbishop asked where he had been educated, Henson replied "I graduated, Your Grace, from the University of Adversity."

In 1849 Henson wrote *The Life of Josiah Henson, formerly a Slave, Now an Inhabitant of Canada.* Harriet Beecher Stowe, an abolitionist from Brooklyn, used Josiah's memoirs as a reference for a book she was writing. *Uncle Tom's Cabin* became one of the greatest selling books in history. Of course it was condemned as false by slave owners. But Mrs. Stowe just kept reminding them about Henson's memoirs.

In later life, Henson became quite wealthy. In fact he grew richer than his former master. In 1877 he toured the United States. He met President Rutherford B. Hayes at the White House and visited the Riley plantation. When old Mrs. Riley saw him, she said, "Why, Sie, you are a gentleman." Henson smiled and replied, "I always was, madam." He died in 1881.

Laura Haviland was a wife, mother, teacher, and conductor on the Underground Railroad.

Laura Haviland was a Quaker, a housewife, and a mother in Ohio, as well as a conductor on the Underground Railroad. Born in 1808, when she was about 12 years old Laura read a book that described the horrors of escaping slavery and became a dedicated abolitionist. As a young woman she opened a school which was revolutionary in admitting boys and girls, blacks and whites, on an equal basis. In 1845, needing help around the school, she hired a young black couple, Willis and Elsie Hamilton. The Hamiltons had six children but when they fled slavery they had been forced to leave two behind. While they were working for Haviland, slave catchers almost managed to grab the Hamiltons by using these two children as bait. It was only by good luck and the help of Haviland and some other people that they were able to avoid capture. This incident inspired Haviland to become involved in the Underground Railroad.

Between 1845 and the outbreak of the Civil War Haviland served as the conductor for many escapes. She often traveled deep into the South, once getting as far as Arkansas. Haviland often used disguises, sometimes quite ingenious ones. She even pretended to be a light-skinned slave, working in the fields, while arranging one escape. Haviland hated slave catchers. Several people whom she helped escape from the South were later recaptured by slave catchers and returned to bondage. Determined that they be free, she went back and helped them escape a second time. She became quite clever at deceiving slave catchers.

Correspondence Along the Underground Railroad

Harriet Tubman

Letter to J. Miller McKim (prominent Pennsylvania abolitionist and conductor on the Underground Railroad) from Thomas Garrett, December 29, 1854.

Esteemed Friend, J. Miller McKim:

We made arrangements last night, and sent away Harriet Tubman, with six men and one woman to Allen Agnew's, to be forwarded across the country to the city. Harriet and one of the men had worn their shoes off their feet, and I gave them two dollars to help fit them out, and directed a carriage to be hired at my expense, to take them out, but do not yet know the expense. I now have two more from the lowest county in Maryland, on the Peninsula, upwards of one hundred miles. I will try to get one of our trusty colored men to take them to-morrow morning to the Anti-slavery office. You can then pass them on.

Thomas Garrett

★ ★ ★

Letter to William Still from Thomas Garrett, December 1, 1860.

Respected Friend: I write to let you know that Harriet Tubman is again in these parts. She arrived last evening from one of her trips of mercy to God's poor, bringing two men with her as far as New Castle. I agreed to pay a man last evening, to pilot them on their way to Chester county; the wife of one of the men, with two or three children, was left some thirty miles below, and I gave Harriet ten dollars, to hire a man with carriage, to take them to Chester county. She said a man had offered for that sum, to bring them on. I shall be very uneasy about them, till I hear they are safe. There is now much more risk on the road, till they arrive here, than there has been for several months past, as we find that some poor, worthless wretches are constantly on the look out on two roads, that they cannot well avoid more especially with carriage, yet, as it is Harriet who seems to have had a special angel to guard her on her journey of mercy, I have hope.

Thy Friend,
Thomas Garrett

Sometimes Laura hid fugitives on their master's own property, while leaving evidence that they had fled. When the search for the fugitives spread far from the plantation, she led the escapees to safety. In order to throw the slave catchers off the trail, she sometimes had fugitives who were living in one state write letters to their former master, apologizing for escaping, and then mailed them from a different state. Once Haviland learned that a free black man from Kentucky had only been pretending to work for the Underground Railroad, while helping the slave catchers for the reward money. She helped spread the rumor that the man was double-crossing the slave catchers, helping more slaves to escape than he was betraying; soon he was no longer a problem.

Haviland became very well-known in abolitionist circles. She worked closely with Levi Coffin, who helped so many people escape from slavery that he sometimes was called the president of the Underground Railroad, and many other notable antislavery activists. Haviland worked on the Underground Railroad despite many personal hardships. The work kept her far from home at times and several of her children died of disease. But she never gave up working to free people.

When the Civil War came, Haviland organized assistance for the many people who fled slavery as Union forces advanced in the Mississippi Valley, and later became an employee of the Freedman's Bureau. In 1881 she wrote *A Woman's Life Work*, about her adventures. Laura Haviland died in 1898.

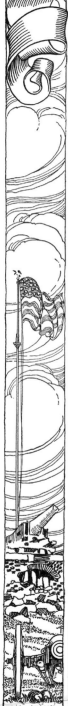

IV

Some Notable Escapes

The story of the Underground Railroad is not only that of the conductors and managers who ran it, brave as they often were. It is even more the story of the very ordinary people who escaped from slavery. There were thousands of them, tens of thousand. All of them had exciting stories to tell. Some of the escapes took place under very unusual circumstances, and often involved great cleverness and much courage. Many stories will never be told, for no one recorded them. But many others are known, and it's worth looking at a few of them.

A Salt Merchant's Boats. Even for the Underground Railroad John Fairfield was an unusual conductor. The son of rich slave owners, he had become a dedicated opponent of slavery. Fairfield helped lead many people to freedom, usually in groups of 20 or more, often displaying wonderful cleverness, usually with great daring, and sometimes in a hail of bullets.

Many slaves fled by boat, as did the groups helped by John Fairfield.

In the mid-1850s Fairfield was asked to arrange the escape of some slaves from northeastern Kentucky. By chance, these people lived near a salt works on the banks of the Kanawha River, not far from where it flowed into the Ohio. So Fairfield, aided by two free black men who courageously masqueraded as his slaves, set himself up as a salt merchant. He ordered two boats be built to transport the salt down the Kanawha River to Ohio. This took some time, of course. While the boats were being built, Fairfield and his "slaves" contacted the people whom they had come to free and made their plans.

One boat was completed first. The escape was planned for a Saturday night. Like many Underground Railroad conductors, Fairfield often staged escapes on Saturdays—slave owners often found it difficult to organize search parties on Sundays. So, Saturday night, half of the people he had come to help sneaked aboard Fairfield's boat. One of Fairfield's "slaves" took the boat down the river towards Ohio. Sunday morning, of course, the slave owners discovered their "property" was missing. Still pretending to be a slave owner, Fairfield joined the search for fugitives and so it was not until Monday morning that he pretended to discover that his boat had been stolen and his slave was missing. Fairfield threw a furious tantrum, yelling and cursing. He abused his remaining "slave." The following week, with the second boat finished, Fairfield sent another batch of people down river to freedom, in the charge of his remaining assistant.

When this newest escape was discovered, Fairfield again joined in the search for the fugitives. He led a search party down the river. Having gone a few miles they spotted one of the boats abandoned on the Ohio side. Fairfield immediately organized a search of the Ohio shoreline. And while the other searchers were occupied, Fairfield quietly slipped away to join his passengers.

John Fairfield helped liberate more than a thousand people from slavery. Called by one historian "an artist in the art of freedom," he disappeared forever in the late 1850s, while on a mission into the slave states.

An Escape Betrayed. Early in 1857 Henry Predo, a slave of Richard Meredith, in Buckstown, Maryland, learned that he was to be "sold South." Predo decided to escape. Working with four other men and two women, Predo was able to contact Thomas Otwell, a black man who worked for the Underground Railroad. Otwell agreed to help the group escape. They fled on March 7. For several days they eluded their pursuers, hiding in barns and woods and marshes. Meanwhile, Meredith posted a $3,000 reward for "the recovery of his property." It was a lot of money in those days, more than a common workman might make in four or five years. The reward proved too tempting for Otwell. He betrayed them to the local sheriff, and together the two laid a trap. About 4:00 on the morning of March 10, Otwell led the fugitives to the back of the Dover County jail. He led them up a flight of stairs, into a darkened room. Suddenly a lamp was lit, revealing bars on the windows and the sheriff and several deputies.

The desperate fugitives fought, beating back the sheriff and his men. They fled down the stairs. Seeing a door, they broke through it into what turned out to be the sheriff's apartment. The sheriff's wife began screaming. The sheriff and his men were close behind. One of the fugitives took a shovel full of hot coals from the fireplace and hurled it at their pursuers. In the confusion, the two women fugitives leaped through an open window. Predo snatched an andiron from the fireplace and smashed the window sash, widening the opening, then leaped through, to be followed by the other men. A quick run across the yard brought them to a fence, over which they fled into the darkness, pursued by the sheriff.

Aided by a local antislavery sympathizer, six of the fugitives were able to reach an Underground Railroad station. After a few days in hiding, arrangements were made to move them further north. Within about two weeks they were in the free states, and they shortly moved on to Canada. The two remaining fugitives also eventually managed to reach safety. So although they had been betrayed, this party of fugitives finally won their freedom. Others were not so lucky.

The Ailing Master and his Faithful Slave. Ellen and William Craft were two young people very deeply in love, and determined to flee slavery in their native Georgia for freedom in the North. William had managed to save a good deal of money, since his master allowed him to work for hire in return for a flat "rental." This helped them to carry out a daring escape. Ellen had a very light complexion and could easily be mistaken for white. William was a large man, much darker than his beloved. They decided to escape disguised as a young master and his personal servant. William's disguise was simple enough, and he was soon dressed as befitted the servant of a rich, young man. Ellen required a bit more of a disguise. With the help of contacts in the Underground Railroad they managed to obtain some fine clothes for her to wear. Soon she was dressed like a frail man suffering from a variety of ills. Her beardless face was concealed partially by dark glasses and partially by a cloth muffler.

Ellen Craft posed as a frail, white man and William Craft posed as "his" slave to travel from the deep South to freedom in the North.

Since she did not know how to write, her right hand was bandaged as if severely injured.

The two made their way to Charleston, South Carolina, where, dressed in their disguises, they checked into one of the better hotels in town. William made all the arrangements. He explained that his master was desperately ill and traveling north for medical treatment. Using the false name and address that William provided, the hotel clerks registered the ill young man and his slave. From Charleston the pair went by rail through South Carolina, North Carolina, and on into Virginia. Along the way William very carefully tended his poor master, politely explaining to inquisitive strangers that the man was very ill and unable to speak to anyone. At Richmond, Virginia, they had to stay overnight, while awaiting a train north. Again they checked into a good hotel. The "ailing master" made his way with great difficulty to their room, escorted by William. William's careful attention, kindness, and concern for his master drew favorable comments from many people. The next day they reached Baltimore. Having settled his master into a nearby chair, William attempted to purchase tickets for Philadelphia. A problem immediately arose. The ticket clerk explained that there was no problem selling a ticket for the ill master but, he went on, under Maryland law William, as a slave, could not be taken out of the state to a free state unless a bond was posted against his return. William didn't have enough money to post a bond. Ellen and William's dream of freedom seemed about to end. Thinking quickly, William told the ticket agent, "My master is in a very delicate state of health. We are afraid he may not be able to hold out until he reaches Philadelphia, where he is going for medical treatment. It's out of the question to post a bond, and he cannot be detained." William's apparent concern, and the pathetic appearance of his "young master" did the trick. The ticket was issued without the necessity of a bond.

Within hours Ellen and William were in Philadelphia, where they were welcomed by many of the leaders of the antislavery movement. Since the publicity surrounding their escape was enormous, Philadelphia was not a safe place for the couple, and they shortly departed for England.

John Henry Hill escaped to Canada and later helped others do the same.

Escaping from the Auction Block.

John Henry Hill, 25 years old, was a married slave in central Virginia with several children. Tall and strong, he was a good worker. So good, in fact, that Hill was allowed to work for wages, of which he was required to pay his master $150 a year. Despite this profitable arrangement, Hill's master decided to sell him. Without telling him anything, the master, John Mitchell, took Hill to Richmond, where a great slave auction was held every New Year's Day. On January 1, 1853, Hill suddenly learned that he was to be sold and refused to cooperate. As he was about to be placed in handcuffs, he fought back. In a desperate fight, he beat off four or five men and escaped into the streets and alleys of the city. But though free of his master, he was still in the middle of slave country. Aided by some sympathetic slaves, he made his way to the home of a merchant who was an agent of the Underground Railroad. Hill stayed hidden in the merchant's home for eight months, all the while in secret contact with his mother and family.

In August, Hill went to Petersburg, about 20 miles south of Richmond, with the help of a forged pass. At

Frank Wanzer and his party are depicted here as they were challenged at the Maryland state line.

Petersburg, a prosperous black freeman who was also a secret agent of the Underground Railroad put Hill up, until further arrangements could be made to get him to freedom. But there had been a leak somewhere, and the slave catchers had gotten word that Hill was in Petersburg. Warned by two white Underground Railroad workers, John Henry Hill returned to Richmond on a forged pass.

While the slave catchers looked for Hill in Petersburg, the Underground Railroad secured him a cabin on a steamboat bound for Philadelphia. Provided with yet another forged pass, Hill made his way to the docks, and boarded the steamer on September 12. Within weeks he was living in Toronto, Canada. From there he was able to arrange the escape of his wife and children, and the family was reunited shortly after Christmas, after nearly a year's separation. John Henry Hill became active in the Underground Railroad assisting many others in their escape.

A Christmas Escape. On Christmas Eve of 1855, Frank Wanzer, a slave from Loudon County, Virginia, received permission to use a wagon with a team of horses, plus two riding horses, in order to take his fiancé, Emily Foster, and a small party of other slaves to visit friends on nearby plantations. This was not unusual, for masters often rewarded their "faithful servants" in this fashion. But Wanzer and his companions—totaling two women and four men—had no intention of returning to their "kindhearted and indulgent owners." Instead of visiting neighboring plantations for a few days, they intended to head north for freedom.

Although it was cold and snowy, they made good time, and within a few days had reached the Maryland state line, near the Cheat River, about 100 miles from home. There they were stopped by a band of six white men and a boy. The men challenged the fugitives to explain what they were doing. Wanzer, who was driving the wagon, attempted to talk his way out of trouble. But it soon became clear that the white men were going to arrest them. The fugitives— the women as well as the men—pulled out knives and pistols that they had hidden away. Meanwhile Wanzer whipped up the horses and fled through the band of white men, as the two fugitives on horseback tried to hold off their pursuers. Pistol shots rang out. As Wanzer and three of his companions sped away to safety in the wagon, the two men on horseback fought it out with the slave catchers. As they too tried to escape, one of the men was hit in the back with buck-

Correspondence Along the Underground Railroad

Letter to William Still from Abigail Goodwin, January 25, 1855.

Dear Friend:

The enclosed ten dollars I have made, earned in two weeks, and of course it belongs to the slaves. It may go for the fugitives, or Carolina slaves, whichever needs it most. I am sorry the fugitives' treasury is not better supplied, if money could flow into it as it does into the Tract Fund; but that is not to be expected.

Will that little boy of seven years have to travel on foot to Canada? There will be no safety for him here. I hope his father will get off. John [Henry] Hill writes very well, considering his few advantages. If plenty of good schools could be established in Canada for the benefit of the fugitives, many bright

Abigail Goodwin

scholars and useful citizens would be added to society. I hope these will be in process of time.

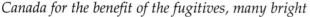

It takes the most energetic and intelligent to make their way out of bondage from the most Southern States. It is rather a wonder to me that so many can escape, the masters are so continually watching them . . . .

A. Goodwin

shot. When the other man turned to try to rescue him, both were captured, and sent back into slavery. The others made their way to freedom by way of the Underground Railroad network.

Frank Wanzer and Emily Foster were married by the Reverend J. W. Logan, the Underground Railroad stationmaster in Syracuse, New York. Soon afterwards the couple settled in Canada. In mid-1856, Wanzer secretly returned to the South to rescue his sister, her husband, and another man from slavery. Having been a passenger on the Underground Railroad, Frank Wanzer became a conductor.

After Lincoln's Emancipation Proclamation many blacks escaped to the Union army's camps.

V

The Underground Railroad in the Civil War

*I*n November of 1860 Abraham Lincoln was elected president. Although he was not an abolitionist, Lincoln had publicly objected to slavery. This made the leaders of some of the slave states fearful that he was going to abolish slavery. So beginning in December of that year, one after another, southern states began passing "Declarations of Secession," in which they proclaimed that since the rest of the nation would not allow them to keep their slaves, they were no longer a part of the United States. By the spring of 1861 the Civil War had broken out, and 11 states—in all of which slaves totaled over 25 percent of the population—had formed the Confederate States of America, a country based on the assumption that slavery was a legitimate, and even moral, institution.

The outbreak of the Civil War did not put an end to the activities of the Underground Railroad but it did change the secret network. New missions arose. The original purpose of the Underground Railroad had been to help people escape from slavery. As a result of

Major General Benjamin F. Butler declared slaves contrabands of war who could be taken into custody by the Union army.

the war escaping became much easier. Very early in the war Union forces ignored the rights of slave owners to claim runaways. In fact, when approached by a slave owner demanding the return of his "property," Major General Benjamin F. Butler declared that slaves were "contraband of war," that is goods that could be confiscated since they were of military value. The phrase "contraband" soon came to be applied to a fugitive slave. Literally hundreds of thousands of people escaped from slavery during the war, fleeing to the nearest Union military forces. By mid-1863 the old mission of the Underground Railroad had largely disappeared; late in that year Thomas Garrett observed that only a handful of fugitive slaves had passed through his station since the war began.

But if they were no longer needed to help slaves escape, the workers on the Underground Railroad still found many jobs that needed to be done. Early in the war they began to help white people escape from the slave states. In much of the South there were many whites who opposed the Confederacy. These people soon found themselves in great danger from supporters of secession. Unionists were sometimes lynched or beaten. Some white Unionists in places like Tennessee eventually found their way to safety in the North through the services of the Underground Railroad.

Meanwhile, many people who had worked for the Underground Railroad became prominent in the war

William Seward fought many court cases involving escaped slaves and later was made Lincoln's secretary of state.

against the Confederacy. William Seward, the "attorney general" of the Underground Railroad, who had fought many court cases in defense of fugitives, became secretary of state in Lincoln's cabinet. Julia Ward Howe, the coeditor of the abolitionist magazine *Commonwealth*, wrote the words to the famous Civil War song, "The Battle Hymn of the Republic," which focused on the war as a struggle for liberation. Frederick Douglass, one of the most famous fugitive slaves, who had sheltered hundreds of other escapees in his home in Rochester, New York, urged President Lincoln to enlist black soldiers, and then, when the president agreed, urged black men to volunteer, among them his sons. William Still, who had helped run the Philadelphia depot of the Underground Railroad, and later wrote the book *The Underground Rail Road*, helped create the Freedman's Association, which arranged housing, jobs, and education for hundreds of fugitive slaves. Other Underground Railroad workers joined the army, to fight against slavery with weapons. Some of these men rose to high rank. David B. Birney, for example, the son of an Alabama slave owner who had sold his slaves and become a prominent abolitionist, became a Union general.

Underground Railroad conductors worked for the Union as guides and scouts. The most famous was Harriet Tubman. Soon after the Union army captured the Sea Islands, off the Carolina coast, Tubman went there to work as a nurse for the freedmen and Union soldiers. In June of 1863, Colonel James Montgomery, commander of the 2nd North Carolina, a black regiment, asked her to accompany an expedition up the Combahee River. The troops were to travel by gunboat up the river, in order to remove mines that blocked navigation and to gather supplies, while helping slaves to escape. The expedition departed on the night of June 2. It was wildly successful. Not only were portions of the river cleared of mines, but a lot of supplies were collected. And, best of all, Tubman's presence with the expedition encouraged the local slaves to seek their freedom. As a result, over 750 people—men, women, and children—fled slavery and were brought to safety. Many of the newly liberated men soon joined the army and fought against slavery.

Julia Ward Howe worked on the abolitionist magazine Commonwealth. *She was the author of the lyrics of the famous Civil War song "The Battle Hymn of the Republic" which focused on the struggle for freedom.*

During the war former slaves and Underground Railroad workers often used many of their escape techniques to further the Union cause. Secret hiding places that had once sheltered fugitive slaves were used to hide spies or Union soldiers who were escaping capture. Some Underground Railroad workers became spies for the Union. For example, in February 1862, the Union navy was concerned about an iron-clad warship that the Confederates were building in Norfolk, Virginia. The navy was able to obtain information on the ship from Mrs. Mary Touveste. A free black woman, Mrs. Touveste obtained employment at the home of one of the Confederate officers supervising the construction of the ship at the Norfolk Navy Yard. She stole some plans and documents about the

David B. Birney, who had worked on the Underground Railroad prior to the Civil War, became a prominent Union general even though he was from the Confederate state of Alabama.

new vessel (the famous *Merrimack* or *Virginia*). Then she made her way to Washington by means of the Underground Railroad.

Methods of concealing messages that had been used by Underground Railroad agents to pass information about escape plans—such as hiding notes in loaves of bread—were used to carry military information to Union generals. A notable example of the use of an old Underground Railroad technique occurred in the spring of 1863. At that time the Union and Confederate armies were in a stalemate, facing each other across the Rappahannock River, near Fredericksburg in northern Virginia. A black couple named

Dabney were serving as spies for the Union army. Mrs. Dabney was working as a cook and laundress at the headquarters of a Confederate general, on the south side of the river. She was in a good position to overhear important information. Mrs. Dabney would communicate with Mr. Dabney using a clothesline— by hanging clothes of different colors in different patterns she alerted her husband to Confederate movements. He would then pass that information on to the Union army. This was a technique that had been used by Underground Railroad agents to identify stations and to alert fugitives as to whether it was safe or not safe for them to approach.

So the people of the Underground Railroad labored on through the Civil War, until slavery had been eliminated. And even then, some of them continued to work. After the war people like Harriet Tubman, Thomas Garrett, Frederick Douglass, Laura Haviland, and many other former Underground Railroad workers continued to struggle for freedom and equality.

Many Union soldiers were helped by slaves when they needed refuge during the war. These slaves often used the methods and safe houses of the Underground Railroad.

★ ★ ★

From time to time in history organizations similar to the Underground Railroad have existed. The escape lines that helped Allied prisoners-of-war, Jewish people, and anti-Nazis flee German-dominated Europe during World War II come to mind, as well as the complex networks that have often been established to support revolutionary movements in some countries. But for sheer scale, duration, and dedication, there is really nothing in history that compares with the Underground Railroad. For nearly 200 years thousands of men and women of different races, religions, and classes worked together in the face of great odds and enormous danger to help free people from oppression.

The Underground Railroad is not just a story about America and Americans, but one that stands as an example to all humanity of what people of goodwill and courage can accomplish to right injustices.

Glossary

abolitionist movement
A movement of people who worked for the abolishment of slavery.

attorney general of the Underground Railroad
Sometimes used to describe William Seward, because of the many times he appeared in court in defense of runaway slaves.

"Box" Brown
Nickname applied to Henry Brown after his famous escape from slavery in a wooden crate.

conductor
Someone who served as a guide for people escaping from slavery.

contraband
A nickname applied to fugitive slaves during the Civil War, in reference to Benjamin F. Butler's 1861 declaration. He claimed slaves were valuable property likely to be of use to the enemy, so they could be confiscated as "contraband of war."

depot
Used to describe the northern terminals of the Underground Railroad.

freedman/ freedwoman
A person who had been formally freed from slavery.

freedom papers
Legal documents issued to persons who had been freed from slavery.

Fugitive Slave Law of 1793
A federal law that said slaveowners had the right to pursue fugitives into free states, but that did not require federal officials to cooperate in the search for the escapees.

Fugitive Slave Law of 1850
A federal law that required federal and state officials to lend assistance to persons pursuing fugitive slaves.

laying out	When fugitives hid out near their former master's property, in order to keep in touch with family and friends, rather than continue north.
"Moses"	The nickname applied to Harriet Tubman, who, like Moses in the Bible, guided her people out of slavery.
passengers	Commonly used to describe people who were traveling on the Underground Railroad.
slave catchers	People who made their living recapturing fugitive slaves.
station	A safe place where fugitives could hide while waiting to proceed on the next leg of their journey to freedom.
stationmaster	Someone who ran a station.
stockholder	Anyone who supported the Underground Railroad with money and goods.

Further Reading

The most important book ever written about the Underground Railroad is William Still's *The Underground Rail Road*. Originally published in Philadelphia in 1872, it has been reprinted many times since. It is based on original documents, including Still's own files as an official of the Pennsylvania Anti-Slavery Society, as well as his interviews with escaped slaves, and letters that came into his possession. Unlike most of the people who have written on the subject since Still's book appeared, he concentrated on the story that the fugitives themselves had to tell, rather than on the organizers and leaders of the antislavery movement. Unfortunately, Still concentrated on those who escaped from slavery to such an extent that he failed to provide even an outline history of how the Underground Railroad was organized and functioned.

The second most valuable book on the subject is Wilbur H. Siebert's *The Underground Railroad from Slavery to Freedom*, first issued in New York in 1898 and also reprinted several times. Siebert's book was based on interviews with fugitives and former Underground Railroad workers, as well as upon surviving documents. His focus is more on the Underground Railroad as an organization, loose as it may have been.

There are several recent books about slavery and the Underground Railroad that younger readers may find of interest:

Bentley, Judith. *"Dear Friend," Thomas Garrett & William Still: Collaborators on the Underground Railroad*. New York: Dutton, 1997.

Blockson, Charles L. *Hippocrene Guide to the Underground Railroad*. New York: Hippocrene, 1994.

Collison, Gary. *Shadrach Minkins: From Fugitive Slave to Citizen*. Cambridge, Mass.: Harvard University Press, 1998.

Douglass, Frederick. *The Autobiography of Frederick Douglass*.

Evitts, William J. *Captive Bodies, Free Spirits: The Story of Southern Slavery*. New York: Julian Messner, 1985.

Gara, Larry. *The Liberty Line: The Legend of the Underground Railroad*. Lexington: University of Kentucky Press, 1961.

Hamilton, Virginia. *Many Thousand Gone: African Americans from Slavery to Freedom*. New York: Knopf, 1993.

Petry, Ann. *Harriet Tubman: Conductor on the Underground Railroad*. New York: Harper: 1996.

Websites About the Underground Railroad

Harriet Tubman: http://www2.1hric.org/pocantico/tubman/tubman.html

National Park Service Sites: http://www.nps.gov/undergroundrr

North Star Foundation: http://www.Underground Railroad.org/

The Underground Railroad: http://www.niica.on.ca/csonan/UNDERGROUND.htm

A Walk to Canada: http://www.npca.org/

Index

PHOTO CREDITS
Underground Rail Road by William Still: pp. 10, 16, 18, 23, 25, 26, 33, 40, 43, 45, 46, 48; *Illustrated London News*: p. 13; Library of Congress: pp. 15, 20, 30; National Archives: pp. 28, 34, 37, 55; *Harper's Weekly*: 50, 52, 53, 56, 57